The Authorpreneur Handbook
Building an Abundant Life for Feminist, Queer, and BIPOC Writers

Angela Yarber

TEHOM CENTER

WWW.TEHOMCENTER.ORG

Copyright © 2024 by Angela Yarber Ph.D.

All rights reserved.

No part of this book may be reproduced in any form or by any electronic or mechanical means, including information storage and retrieval systems, without written permission from the author, except for the use of brief quotations in a book review.

Tehom Center Publishing is a 501(c)3 nonprofit publishing feminist and queer authors, with a commitment to elevate BIPOC writers. Its face and voice is Rev. Dr. Angela Yarber.

Paperback ISBN: 978-1-966655-00-8

Ebook ISBN: 978-1-966655-01-5

Contents

Acknowledgments — vii
A Note about Stories — ix

1. Introduction — 1
2. A Creative Caveat — 7
3. Book Doula Writing — 11
4. Book Diva Marketing — 43
5. Book DreamMaker Authorpreneur — 91

Aligning With Your Activism — 115
Conclusion — 119

Dedicated to the revolutionary writers at Tehom Center Publishing

Acknowledgments

As always, writing a book takes a village, and my village is filled with some really fabulous people. I'm grateful for generous beta readers, Diana McLean, Katy Valentine, and Emily Hedrick, a wonderful editor, and for the supportive community at Tehom Center Publishing. Working with a publishing company, a press publishing feminist and queer authors, with a commitment to elevate BIPOC writers, who shares my values is a gift I relish.

For the authors and clients who have entrusted me with authorpreneurship coaching, daring to leave the traditional, the 9-5, the toxic, the discriminatory to leap into the unknown of authorpreneurship, thank you. The way you're living your dreams inspires and emboldens me. I am thankful for the revolutionary writers in TCP's cohorts, Ministry from the Margins Books, and one-on-one coaching clients.

For friends, family, colleagues, and communities who nurture this writing and authorpreneur life, I give thanks: my team, St. Pete Girl Bosses, YCW Alum, retreatants, doctoral students, and PhD colleagues.

My parents, little brother, wife, and children top my list of gratitude. Elizabeth, I appreciate your support of my endless processing, your nearly tireless belief in my work, that you had the courage and audacity to come work *with* me, and the ways you patiently and lovingly nurture our family so that this authorpreneur life can be possible. You make this dreamy life even better, more just, and more hilarious. I love you and thank you.

And for you, dear readers, I am grateful that you're questioning the status quo. Thank you for your commitment to dismantling the belief that marginalized writers are meant to remain on the margins, for questioning the "struggling writer" myth, and for demanding an equitable and abundant life that honors your creativity, craft, and calling. That's what the authorpreneur life is all about. Thanks for allowing me to be your co-conspirator in crafting the life of your dreams.

A Note about Stories

Throughout *The Authorpreneur Handbook,* you'll encounter myriad stories about writers who achieved the writing life of their dreams. To protect the anonymity of my clients and authors, I've chosen to write vignettes inspired by my clients, combining different elements of their stories rather than using direct testimonials or client names. Testimonials are available on the back cover of this book and on Tehom Center Publishing's website and social media.

www.tehomcenter.org

Introduction

"The world I create in my writing compensates for what the real world does not give me."

— *Gloria Anzaldúa*

I DIDN'T EVEN KNOW about the term authorpreneur when I became one, mostly because I didn't yet consider myself an entrepreneur.

Author + Entrepreneur = Authorpreneur.

Over a decade ago, after protests from Westboro Baptist Church, a thick stack of hate mail, and even a few death threats, I decided two institutions had become too toxic for me as a queer woman. The first was the church. Interestingly, I was its pastor. Yep, a queer woman like me was a pastor. Weird, I know. But there are more of us than you'd think. The second was the academy where I was a professor. I'd spent nearly fifteen years tied to those institutions. But they became too much, too confining, too exclusive, too toxic.

So, I left to traverse the American landscape in a pop-up camper named Freya, wife and toddler in tow, for nearly two years, discerning my next vocational steps by researching and heeding the wisdom of revolutionary queer women of color. I wrote all about it in my last book, *Queering the American Dream*. In the ten intervening years, I published eight award-winning books with four different publishing companies. I realized, however, that most independent publishing companies don't understand the nuances of what it means to be a feminist or queer writer; they certainly don't know how to market us. I'd connected myself to yet another toxic institution. And making a living as a writer seemed out of reach.

You're probably aware of the starving artist or struggling writer stereotype. That's what I thought and believed for a long time. That you can't make a living as a writer. That being a writer isn't practical. It's not a way to pay the bills. And that's what this book is out to debunk. Particularly for marginalized writers.

Around the same time, two dear friends and colleagues—who are both smart, savvy, marginalized businesswomen—each spent over $40,000 (yes, you read that correctly) on a hybrid publishing company promising to help them write and publish a book, leveraging said book to build a million-dollar business. Both friends are now over $40,000 in debt and those businesses don't even exist anymore because they never made enough to cover their initial investment. That's because they signed with what I believe was a predatory publishing company. And what makes publishing companies like that so egregious is that they prey upon marginalized women with the promise of riches.

One of my favorite writers and ancestors is Gloria Anzaldúa, a queer Chicana feminist from the borderlands of Mexico and Texas who claimed: "The world I create in my writing compensates for what the real world does not give me."

The "real world" has given us an old-school, white, male, predatory publishing industry that, at best, doesn't understand the nuances of queer, feminist, antiracist writing, and at worst, preys upon us for capital gain. Hear me clearly. Not *all* publishing companies are bad and toxic. Some are fabulous. Most, however, are not attuned to the needs and nuances of marginalized writers. So, I created Tehom Center Publishing to compensate for what the real world has not given us. Tehom Center Publishing is a press publishing feminist and queer authors, with a commitment to elevate BIPOC writers. Tehom Center Publishing does not charge a single penny for authors to publish with us.

However, we acknowledge that many authors need some guidance and coaching along the way, so we provide those services for equitable fees. This book is a result of coaching over one hundred authorpreneurs thus far and seeing them succeed. I don't want access to these methods to be limited to those who can afford 1:1 or group coaching, though. I want them to be accessible to everyone, whether you buy this book or check it out from your local library for absolutely free. Money should never prevent a writer from pursuing publishing dreams. That's precisely what keeps marginalized writers at the margins.

This *Authorpreneur Handbook* guides you through the process of writing and marketing your book so that you can live the authorpreneur life of your dreams, particularly if you are a marginalized person. The exercises and information in this handbook provide the exact template I use to coach authors at Tehom Center Publishing. Now, I'm sharing them with you!

Who am I and what business do I have coaching you through your authorpreneur journey?

I'm Dr. Ang, author of eight award-winning books that have been featured in *Forbes*, *HuffPo*, *Ms. Magazine*, *NPR*, the *Advocate*, the television show Tiny House Nation, and more. After publishing eight books with four different publishing companies, I realized that most presses don't understand the nuances of publishing and marketing feminist and queer authors.

I'm also an enneagram 1, Myers Briggs INTJ, Leo sun, Cancer rising queer mama of two foster-to-adopt kiddos with disabilities who does, indeed, enjoy long walks on the beach. Forest bathing and hiking are fabulous, too. Painting and writing became my deep, abiding joy and creative outlets around the time I retired from dancing professionally at age 30. And empowering other marginalized creatives to live the life of their dreams is pretty much what drives me.

I knew that I wasn't alone in being marginalized within the publishing industry, but that countless other women, BIPOC, queer folks, and other historically marginalized people must also be experiencing the inaccessibility of, not only the publishing industry, but of achieving financial abundance by doing what you love: writing. And I also experienced the transformation of unlocking the magic of living the authorpreneur life.

I literally went from living significantly below the poverty line and relying on government assistance to more than quintupling my income, breaking that sought-after six figure mark (and more!), and realizing financial sustainability while doing what I love—writing—in a way that makes a difference in the world. Living such a life wasn't enough for me, though.

I wanted to help other marginalized authors live their dream lives, as well. I wanted to empower marginalized authors who are dedicated to global change to achieve the abundant life we work so hard to create for others.

Did you know that only 16% of published books are written by LGBTQIA+ authors? Even worse, only 11% are by BIPOC writers! These are the perspectives and stories the world needs most. So, I created Tehom Center Publishing to offer a corrective. Tehom Center Publishing is a press publishing feminist and queer authors, with a commitment to elevate BIPOC writers.

Through Tehom Center Publishing, I have the privilege of coaching authors, not only in book writing, but in strategic book marketing and leveraging a book to build a brand and business so that marginalized authors can live a life of abundance. For too long, people at the margins haven't had access to sharing our stories, publishing our books, and accessing financial abundance so that we can truly thrive. Tehom Center Publishing wants to change this.

If you want to write and publish a book, market your book for maximum reach, and build the authorpreneur life of your dreams, keep reading. Follow this step-by-step guide that has informed my coaching of authors who have left full-time jobs to live the creative life, created an off-ramp from toxic positions in the academy, the church, and corporate America, become #1 Amazon bestsellers, and experienced their books featured in top media and publications. Now, I'm sharing it with you.

How to Use *The Authorpreneur Handbook*

The Authorpreneur Handbook is divided into three sections:

1. Book Doula Writing
2. Book Diva Marketing
3. Book DreamMaker Authorpreneur

In each section there are exercises to complete. It's vital to the process that you complete each exercise in order before moving to the next. This is a handbook, so feel free to write directly in the book. Use your favorite pen. Color code your highlighters. Do whatever makes you happy and provides as much clarity as possible in this handbook.

I recommend flipping through the entire handbook before getting started to give you a glimpse at what you're getting into. In the Book Doula Writing chapter, our exercises are aimed at addressing the WHY, WHAT, and WHEN of writing your book. The Book Diva Marketing chapter introduces you to The Power of 50 in marketing, guiding you through creating your ultimate launch team, pitching media, and crafting fun ideas that align marketing with your intersectionally feminist values. And the Book DreamMaker Authorpreneur chapter leverages the WHY of your book to create a business funnel so you can financially live the writer life of your dreams.

Each chapter also includes some exercises surrounding mindset, along with calendaring so that all the lists you create have doable due dates affixed to them for maximum impact. Plus, chapters also include opportunities for reflection and celebration. Marginalized writers need and deserve more affirming spaces for rest and joyous celebration, so please be sure to pause, reflect, and celebrate each step along the way. Because what you're doing—writing and marketing a book and developing an authorpreneur business—is a really big deal worthy of celebration!

After you've completed the handbook, you'll have A LOT of lists, doable due dates, and strategic plans for writing, marketing, and launching your funnel. I'll admit that it is a lot to manage and can become a bit overwhelming. To aid you in streamlining your process, I've narrowed all these fabulous exercises into a simple one-pager that you can glance at and be reminded of the big picture of your book and business. It's best to complete this one pager *after* you've finished all the exercises in the handbook, but I recommend you go ahead and download it now so you have a roadmap for your authorpreneur journey.

You can download it simply at www.tehomcenter.org/handbook.

Download and print it. Once you've finished all your exercises, fill it in and hang it where you write as a visual and tangible reminder of your revolutionary work.

And here's some amazing news. Living the authorpreneur life of your dreams is a possibility for all marginalized writers. It may be that you adore your day job, but also adore writing; maybe you don't want an off ramp from your 9-5. But writing on the side and earning even more income in the process can't hurt. The authorpreneur life is possible for you. Maybe you absolutely loathe your job and cannot wait for the moment when you can quit, but you need the steady paycheck or access to health insurance. The authorpreneur life can supplement and then replace your current paycheck so that you don't have to stay in a toxic work environment. Whether you want writing to be your part-time, your full-time, your right now, your forever, or anywhere in between, living the authorpreneur life of your dreams is waiting for you.

I believe a better world is possible, a world where the voices on the margins are brought to the center, where all people have access to abundance, beauty, and joy. Join me in creating such a world. Join me in writing toward the authorpreneur life!

A Creative Caveat
Contemplative Coloring

You may be scratching your head when you see a coloring page at the start of an authorpreneur handbook. What does drawing and coloring have to do with writing and publishing? Well, you're welcome to skip this exercise if it's too "woowoo" for you, but I encourage you to try. Utilizing color, design, and even writing in different directions on unlined paper taps into different parts of our brains than linear writing does. It has the potential to unlock writing ideas in ways similar to walking, hiking, running, yoga, or washing the dishes. Truly, how many times have you gotten your most brilliant writing idea while washing your hair in the shower or walking the dog?

So, I invite you to use this drawing to unlock some otherwise closed portions of your brain. As you color or write in the **heart**, consider what the heart of your book is. While writing or coloring the **hair**, imagine what wisdom pours forth from your brilliant **mind**. When your colored pencils or markers or crayons fill in the **book**, meditate on the **content** of your writing. And in the space surrounding this book goddess, imagine in color, word, and design the transformative **impact** your book will have on the world.

This is the only exercise that you don't need to complete before moving to the next section. Rather, this creative caveat is an artistic opportunity you can return to time and again throughout this handbook. Or if you're totally jazzed, you can complete it in one sitting. You do you.

I've had a client complete different sections of the coloring page as a "reward" after finishing each exercise or meeting a doable due date with her writing. Others have sat down with gel pens, watercolors, markers, crayons, and colored pencils and had an arty party as a way to contemplatively honor the beginning of this authorpreneur journey. Still others waited until finishing all the exercises and celebrated by returning to the Book Goddess.

A few have matted and framed her, hanging the art in their writing spaces as a visual and tangible reminder of their authorpreneur journey. I personally return to her with each writing project, invoking the wisdom of my ancestors and spiritual guides who inform my writing. Because writing, especially for those of us who exist at the margins, can be a sacred act. It's an act of compensation, like Anzaldúa reminds us, an act of imagining a better world, a revolutionary act.

And sometimes revolution requires colored pencils. So, tap into the heart, wisdom, content, and impact of your book, and sharpen those pencils.

Heart = *heart* of your writing
Hair = *wisdom* of your writing
Book = *content* of your writing
Open space = *impact* of your writing

If it emboldens your process, share a photo of your completed Book Goddess on socials with #authorpreneurhandbook

Tehom Center Publishing

Book Doula Writing

> *"If there's a book you want to read, but it hasn't been written yet, then you must write it."*
>
> — *Toni Morrison*

IN ORDER TO WRITE A BOOK, you must know the WHY, WHAT, and WHEN behind your writing. We begin with the WHY.

Acclaimed Black American novelist and academic, Toni Morrison, reminds us that our needs, our desires, our WHY drives writing a book.

Let me tell you about Sage.

Sage's Why Statement

Sage was a queer coach who helped marginalized women process trauma and how such trauma blocked their transformative work in the world. Her work was revolutionary, empowering, inspiring, and absolutely exhausting. She worked with at least eight different clients per day in one-on-one coaching calls and she was undercharging. Yes, she was making a tremendous difference in the lives of her clients, but she didn't have the capacity to reach more people because her days were filled with coaching sessions, and she was too emotionally spent at the end of the day to do anything else. She knew writing a book would help her reach more people, but she couldn't focus on what exactly to write about.

Enter the Book Doula Coaching Program. Sage knew she wanted to make a difference in the lives of other marginalized women, but she kept getting caught up in the WHAT behind her book rather than letting the WHY drive her. Once Sage let the WHY—empowering marginalized women—fuel her writing, she found clarity on what she needed to write about. She invited her clients' stories of transformation to provide the framework of her book. Every time she battled writer's block, she looked above her desk at her bulletin board where she wrote and hung her Why Statement and the words that spilled from her teal glitter pen unleashed her inner writing goddess.

You see, Sage had been empowering marginalized women for nearly a decade. She simply needed to recount her stories, outline her framework for transformation, and put those experiences into words. Returning again and again to her Why Statement gave her the clarity she needed to write and publish her book. Along the way, I also encouraged her to double her prices, reduce her client load, and add a group cohort so she could expand her reach. Combined with the number of marginalized women who discovered her work by reading her book, Sage now works a reasonable workday that isn't overflowing with underpaying clients. She's empowering even more women and making even more money, alleviating so much of the stress she experienced before the writing and publishing of her book.

Discovering her WHY transformed Sage's life and work.

Having an idea for a book is one thing. Knowing why, what, and when you're writing it is another.

Did you know that over 80% of Americans claim to *want* to write a book? Yet less than 0.5% actually write and publish one! Why?

Most people lack the resources and know how to make it happen. That's what this section of *The Authorpreneur Handbook* is giving you. Reading about and doing exercises surrounding the WHY, WHAT, and WHEN of your book will help you create a strategy to transform your book concept into an actual finished manuscript.

Remember to read each section and complete each exercise fully before moving to the next section.

WHY
Why are you writing?

Knowing your WHY is the most important part of writing a book. Because book writing and publishing is hard. Sometimes it's lonely. And you need a constant reminder of WHY you're doing this. So, why is this topic important to you? Why does it matter in the world?

The reasons can range from practical to prophetic.

Practical reasons could include anything from checking off an item on your bucket list to proving your 8th grade English teacher wrong, creating a business lead magnet, or to becoming famous. Having clarity surrounding your practical WHY helps you set expectations for yourself and your book.

But the prophetic WHY is the reason that really gets to the heart of why you're doing what you're doing. When I say prophet, I'm not necessarily talking about someone who predicts the future or speaking of divination or something "woowoo," though if that's your vibe, fabulous.

Rather, prophets have historically been people—often within the world's spiritual traditions—who spoke truth to power, activists who called out injustice and worked for transformative change in the world. So, a prophetic WHY is rooted in systemic change. Prophetic reasons are likely some iteration of making a difference in the world and fulfilling your calling. Do you want to make the church safer for trans people? Do you want marginalized women to accept and celebrate their bodies, no matter the size? Do you want entrepreneurs to realize that having ADHD may be their superpower rather than a weakness?

Exercise:

Take 5 minutes to write freely about WHY you want to write this book.

Now take 3 deep breaths and reread what you wrote. Return to your writing by narrowing down the paragraph into one concise WHY Statement. If fancy font or markers enliven you, write this WHY Statement in an aesthetically pleasing way and hang it somewhere you will always see it as a tangible and visual reminder of why you're writing this book.

My WHY Statement:

WHAT
What are you writing about?

Now that you know WHY you're writing, you need to decide WHAT exactly you're writing about.

Juanita's Word Cloud

Juanita was no stranger to writing and publishing books. In fact, she was a botany professor who had published an introductory botany textbook, in addition to writing a fascinating deep dive into the interconnectedness of tree root systems. As a Mexican American immigrant who was raised in her abuela's sprawling herb garden, mixing herbal remedies for everything from sore throats to menopausal hot flashes, Juanita felt stifled by the academy, her creativity always secondary to lab research. She wanted to write a book about the ways creativity and botany intersect, but when she pitched this idea to her publisher and department chair, they balked. Not scientific enough, they said.

Creativity continued to call Juanita.

With a ceramic pot of oregano on one side and cilantro on the other, she set her lab notes to the side one evening and opened her journal. With her daughter asleep in the neighboring bedroom, Juanita poured her crayons on the table. She began to make a word cloud. Every word or phrase related to botany and creativity that she could think of filled the page, along with sketches of plants, root systems, and flowers. The biggest themes that she knew would occupy multiple chapters were encased in crimson maple leaves. The portions of the research that lend themselves to thick, descriptive details, she surrounded in light green leaves and the tiny purple flowers of lavender. For nearly an hour, Juanita filled the page with words, color, and design. When she paused to review her work, she was shocked.

The word cloud didn't become a tidy, scientific outline for another academic work of nonfiction. Instead, in her word cloud, Juanita was transported back to her abuela's garden, and she had a revelation. The book stirring inside her wasn't another academic text. It wasn't even another work of nonfiction. It was a novel. The research, drawings, and words became characters, plotlines, scenes, and a narrative arc that brought together the two worlds that the academy believed existed separately from one another.

Juanita ended up writing an award-winning novel that fused her research on the interconnectedness of tree root systems with her childhood experiences in her abuela's garden into a creative fantasy world she created. Dr. Juanita didn't want to leave her professorship because she loved her students, but writing and publishing her novel not only honored her creative side, it also opened new worlds for her to speak about the connections between science and creativity. Believe it or not, the chair of her department quickly got on board when he witnessed the success of Juanita's book. Now, she is a professor, authorpreneur, and scientist, honoring every part of herself.

Exercise

WHAT Word Cloud: Create a Word Cloud about WHAT you're writing about.

Jot down everything that comes to mind. Write some words bigger if they're more important, or circle, underline, or *star* them. Draw connecting lines between the words or use different fonts to indicate subtopics (cursive, capitals, lowercase, etc).

Once you have a general idea—a Word Cloud—about what you're writing about, it's time for some market research.

What sets you apart from other authors writing about this topic?

Identity, expertise, experience, angle, enthusiasm?

Do market research with some simple internet searches. What similar books already exist? How is your book going to be different? How will it fill a need in the market? What sets YOU apart as an author?

Exercise:

After doing at least 30 minutes of market research, make a list of ways you and your book will be *different* from the existing books on the topic.

For example, are all the authors writing about this topic white men? Are all the books on this topic directed at academics rather than lay audiences? What sets YOU and your book apart?

Existing Books on This Topic: How is Your Book Different?

1.

2.

3.

4.

5.

6.

Empowered by your market research, return to your WHAT Word Cloud and begin to narrow it into a book thesis statement. Allow The Power of the 5-Paragraph Essay to inspire you.

Angela Yarber

The Power of the 5-Paragraph Essay

In 5th grade you probably learned to write a 5-paragraph persuasive essay. Writing a book is like writing a really long 5-Paragraph essay!

"In this paper/book, I will show [your main argument] by/because [reason 1], [reason 2], and [reason 3]."

For example, I remember a kid in my 8th grade class who decided to write his persuasive essay about ferrets. Yes, mine was on "Focusing on Animal's Rights and Human Wrongs," raging against animal testing, but I was a weird, activist middle schooler.

The 8th grader said simply, "In this paper, I will show that ferrets are the best pets because 1) they are cute, 2) cuddly, and 3) low maintenance."

Those 3 key points became the 3 sections of his essay:

I. Introduction
II. Ferrets are CUTE (paragraph 1)
III. Ferrets are CUDDLY (paragraph 2)
IV. Ferrets are LOW MAINTENANCE (paragraph 3)
V. Conclusion

Exercise:

Take a few minutes to winnow your WHAT Word Cloud into one, clear thesis statement with embedded sub-statements to help create an outline for your book.

*Note: You don't have to limit yourself to exactly 3 reasons or sections. Your "5-Paragraph Essay" may be more of a "7-Paragraph Essay" or "4-Paragraph Essay." Just use the 5-Paragraph Essay as a guide with each body paragraph becoming a section or chapter of your book.

For example, if I was writing a book about Tehom Center Publishing, my thesis might look something like this:

"In this book I will show that a feminist and queer publishing agency is necessary because it 1) dismantles white supremacist cisheteropatriarchy, 2) feminist and queer authors are

underrepresented in the publishing world, and 3) the world would be a better place with more feminist and queer books."

This thesis becomes the foundation of your outline.

> I. Introduction
> II. Dismantling white supremacist cisheteropatriarchy
> III. Feminist and queer authors are underrepresented in publishing
> IV. The world is better with more feminist and queer books
> V. Conclusion

Within each section of your outline (5-Paragraph essay), you add sub-sections (smaller 5-Paragraph essays).

For example:

"We dismantle white supremacist cisheteropatriarchy by defining white supremacy, defining cisheteropatriarchy, explaining its pitfalls, explaining the power of the published word, and envisioning a world without it."

Dividing that into your outline looks like this:

> II. Dismantling white supremacist cisheteropatriarchy
>   a. Defining white supremacy
>   b. Defining cisheteropatriarchy
>   c. Explaining the pitfalls of white supremacist cisheteropatriarchy
>   d. Explaining the power of the published word
>   e. Envisioning a world without white supremacist cisheteropatriarchy

And within each sub-section, there are examples, facts, stories, and more (even smaller 5-Paragraph essays). These may simply be ideas, notes, or personal stories you recollect.

For example:

"In order to help understand what white supremacy is, I will share a personal example, statistics about it, poems and art addressing it, provide a literary review of books discussing it, and conclude by providing methods for addressing it."

Dividing that into your outline looks like this:

II. Dismantling white supremacist cisheteropatriarchy
   a. Defining white supremacy
      i. Personal story about white supremacy
      ii. Statistics about and examples of white supremacy
      iii. Poems and art addressing white supremacy
      iv. Books about white supremacy
      v. Methods for addressing white supremacy

Note: You do NOT have to follow this outline exactly. You may have five main points or sections. Or two. Nuance the thesis statement and outline to suit you. And, yes, it can work for a novel or book of poetry because you still need sections to fill your narrative arc and themes, so creating a thesis statement and outline is essential to know where your book is going.

Exercise:

Divide your thesis statement into an outline.

In this book, I will show...

by/because...

1:

2:

and 3:

Start simple:

>   I. Introduction
>   II. Section One (thesis topic one)
>   III. Section Two (thesis topic two)
>   IV. Section Three (thesis topic three)
>   V. Conclusion

(Add more sections if needed)

Introduction

What big question or problem does your book address?

What unique perspective or solution are you offering?

What essential background will readers need?

Section 1 (Thesis Topic 1)

What's the heart of this section?

Now identify 3-5 main subtopics that help reveal or develop this idea.

    Subtopic 1:

        Now break that down into 3-5 supporting ideas:

    Subtopic 2:

        Now break that down into 3-5 supporting ideas:

    Subtopic 3:

        Now break that down into 3-5 supporting ideas:

Section 2 (Thesis Topic 2)

What's the heart of this section?

Now identify 3-5 main subtopics that help reveal or develop this idea.

Subtopic 1:

Now break that down into 3-5 supporting ideas:

Subtopic 2:

Now break that down into 3-5 supporting ideas:

Subtopic 3:

Now break that down into 3-5 supporting ideas:

Section 3 (Thesis Topic 3)

What's the heart of this section?

Now identify 3-5 main subtopics that help reveal or develop this idea.

    Subtopic 1:

        Now break that down into 3-5 supporting ideas:

    Subtopic 2:

        Now break that down into 3-5 supporting ideas:

    Subtopic 3:

        Now break that down into 3-5 supporting ideas:

Conclusion

What insights have readers gained?

What's next?

Why does it matter?

Outlining your book may take some time, but it's an important step in writing your manuscript. Even if you only have rough ideas for sections and subsections, write them down to get the ball rolling. If you get stuck, try the Word Cloud exercise for each particular section to help you.

Once you've completed your outline, celebrate!

That's a really big deal.

Add the Math

You may be thinking, "Math?! I thought this was an authorpreneur workbook! No one told me about math!!!" Rest assured that this math is tremendously helpful in mitigating any feelings of overwhelm when looking at your outline or staring at the blank page.

The average book is around 50,000 words. Do not feel beholden to this number! There are novels that are 100,000 words, memoirs that are 70,000, children's books that are 750, and lead magnet business books that are 25,000. You need to choose a length that works for you. But know from the outset that roughly 50,000 is average and a solid goal for outlining your writing progress.

To avoid overwhelm, divide the word count among your outline.

So, a 50,000-word manuscript would look like this:

> I. Introduction (10,000 words)*
>
> II. Dismantling white supremacist cisheteropatriarchy (10,000 words)
>
> III. Feminist and queer authors are underrepresented in publishing (10,000 words)
>
> IV. The world is better with more feminist and queer books (10,000 words)
>
> V. Conclusion (10,000 words)

*Note: Introductions and Conclusions are usually a bit shorter than body chapters, but for the sake of easy math, let's keep everything roughly the same. Do not feel beholden to exact numbers.

Still, writing 10,000 words can be a little overwhelming. Divide further.

> II. Dismantling white supremacist cisheteropatriarchy (10,000 words)
>   a. Defining white supremacy (2,000 words)
>   b. Defining cisheteropatriarchy (2,000 words)
>   c. Explaining the pitfalls of white supremacist cisheteropatriarchy (2,000 words)

      d. Explaining the power of the published word (2,000 words)
      e. Envisioning a world without white supremacist cisheteropatriarchy (2,000 words)

Ok, 2,000 words sounds doable. You can easily write that amount in one day, even one writing session. But let's make it even easier!

  II. Dismantling white supremacist cisheteropatriarchy (10,000 words)
      a. Defining white supremacy (2,000 words)
          i. Personal story about white supremacy (400 words)
          ii. Statistics about and examples of white supremacy (400 words)
          iii. Poems and art addressing white supremacy (400 words)
          iv. Books about white supremacy (400 words)
          v. Methods for addressing white supremacy (400 words)

You can easily write 400 words! That's just a long social media post.

Exercise:

Divide your outline into estimated word counts.

Go back to your outline from our previous exercise and write in word count estimates next to each line.

The Great Cut-and-Paste

Rev. River's Great Cut-and-Paste

Rev. River is a non-binary pastor who is incredibly nourished by contemplative spirituality. They've been a pastor at their current church for six years and, despite experiencing microaggressions and transphobia in the wider world and denomination, they have an affirming community and they're beloved in their church. As a highly introverted person who lives a contemplative life, River is feeling vocationally called away from pastoral ministry simply because preaching every single week and having to be "on" for so many people for so many years has become quite draining.

River knows they're called to help other marginalized people live more contemplative, meditative lives and wants to write a book to help transition their career, while still honoring their ministry and calling. After creating an outline, River's confidence in the book project experienced some overwhelm as they wondered how on earth they could write 50,000 words when they're used to only writing about 2,500 words per week with 2,000ish for their sermon and 500ish for their weekly newsletter. Then River experienced the revelation of The Great Cut and Paste.

River began to review their old sermons and it dawned on them that they'd preached roughly fifteen different sermons about contemplation. Plus, they were a keynote speaker at a contemplation conference hosted by their seminary a couple years prior. River also wrote a few different newsletter columns about the power of contemplative spirituality for the church's newsletter. And then River remembered a robust theological email exchange with a colleague that centered on contemplation as a subversively queer practice, a key component of their book idea. River began cutting and pasting all their previous writings into the corresponding spots in their outline and before they knew it, they'd pasted 37,482 words onto an otherwise blank page.

What?!

Now, some of the pasted material needed a lot of editing to make it better fit into the focus of the book manuscript, but some of it was absolutely perfect as is. Other portions inspired or nuanced new ideas for River and they felt unstuck, celebrating that they quickly transformed that blank cursor on their laptop screen into nearly 40,000 words in one sitting.

You may be thinking, "Well good for Rev. River, but I don't have six years of weekly sermons to draw from." But you do have a variety of other things you've written throughout your lifetime, including, but not limited to:

- Published articles
- Emails
- School papers
- Journal entries
- Social media posts
- Notes to yourself
- Letters
- Sermons
- Speaking engagements
- Lectures
- Blogs
- Transcripts
- You can even draw from lists!

Contemplate each section and subsection of your book, and mine through everything you've ever written. If it has anything to do with the WHAT of your book, cut-and-paste it into your manuscript document. It could be anything from a school research paper to a lengthy email about your topic you wrote your aunt to a social media post. Some items you cut and paste can be used almost exactly as is, adding necessary transitional sentences before and after. Most will need more finesse but are great fodder for getting your book going.

And it should go without saying, of course, that I'm *not* telling you to plagiarize yourself. If you've published something elsewhere and want to cut and paste it into your book, you need to request permission from the publisher first. No matter what, though, you can use previously published work as inspiration, fodder, and framework for this book project.

Exercise:

Cull through your documents, emails, notes, journals, and social media and begin to cut and paste anything relevant to your book into the appropriate sections of the outline.

Start by jotting down a list below of documents and writings that come to mind. Then go through your files (digital and otherwise) and paste them into your manuscript.

What's your word count now?!

Angela Yarber

WHEN
When to Write: Calendaring and Setting Due Dates

When do you have time to write?

Callie's Calendar

Callie is a high school English teacher, and she has five classes of 11th graders in the gifted program. Plus, she's the school's softball coach and faculty advisor for the Gay-Straight Alliance. She's also a co-parent to three foster children and two of her children have disabilities that require weekly therapies and additional support. To say Callie's schedule is busy is an understatement. She has dreamed of writing and publishing a book since she was a teenager, though, and as she celebrates her 40th birthday, she decides this simply must be the year that she makes her dreams a reality.

She creates an outline and knows exactly what she wants to write about. Her WHY is deeply embedded in her bones and drives her to get the job done. The problem is that Callie's schedule is so full and she is so exhausted that she struggles to squeeze in time for her writing. Callie tries setting her alarm for 5am and writing for 90 minutes before waking the children and getting them ready for school. After about 10 days of this, she finds herself dozing off at the dinner table and knows it's simply not doable. She tries writing after school, but the needs of her children continually interrupt her as they require help with homework, chores, rides to and from therapies and activities. When she drops the kids off with her ex-wife for the week, she spends 2 days recovering from exhaustion and then has little creative energy to write in the evening rather than doom-scrolling on social media.

After two days in a row of writing between 5-7pm, Callie pulls out her calendar and begins to brainstorm spaces she can carve out for her writing. She's fairly certain that writing at home during the weeks she has the children just isn't in the cards for her; she's too busy and too tired to muster the energy. And she also wants to relish the time with her kids. Then she realized how much her gifted English students love creative writing and enjoy it when she provides a writing prompt with 25 minutes of uninterrupted writing time, followed by moments to read their writing aloud. A light bulb goes off in Callie's mind.

She works 25-minute creative writing sessions into her lesson plans three times a week and commits to writing herself during those sessions. 25 minutes three times a week is 75 minutes. 75 minutes in five classes is nearly six and a half hours of weekly writing time Callie created! Plus, she commits to writing for a couple hours in the afternoons on the weeks when her children are with their other mom. And since she's a public school teacher, she knows she can use part of her summer to write for longer periods of time. With this plan in place, Callie is able to finish her manuscript in less than six months, achieving her goal of getting her book into the world to celebrate her 40th birthday.

It's no secret that, like Callie, your schedule is busy, so when can you legitimately create the time to write, publish, and market a book?

Authors approach the WHEN question in a variety of different ways. The two methods you're likely most familiar with already, I believe, are not accessible for most marginalized writers. The first involves being able to write all day every day while someone else takes care of all your other responsibilities. Rooted in having a heteronormative 1950s housewife who handles, literally, everything except your writing, you can likely picture an older straight white dude, cigar hanging from his mouth, plucking away on a vintage typewriter in a smoke-filled library while his wife handles the cooking, cleaning, and kids.

Most marginalized writers do not live this reality or have the luxury of writing uninterrupted for hours on end every day while our trad wife delivers our tea, meals, and scotch to our mahogany writing desk. So, I'd like our approach to writing to be a bit more realistic.

The second approach you've likely heard of was popularized by queer author and activist, Glennon Doyle, who rises each morning before 5am to write for a couple hours before her children wake up, relishing the quiet space with a combination of discipline and delight. Maybe that works for you, and if so, that's fabulous. If you're anything like me, you deplore an early morning alarm and want to savor every necessary hour of sleep possible. While this critique doesn't really apply to Glennon, I grow weary of hearing atomic habits bros wax philosophic about 4am wakeups so they can do bootcamp workouts and write uninterrupted before working a 9-5 because they claim to have discipline.

A lot of marginalized people don't have the luxury of having this particular type of discipline without sacrificing our self-care and rest because we're up in the night with sick children, or working double shifts, or so exhausted from minority stress that we need more than 8 hours of sleep in order to survive. So, please, for the love of all that is good and holy, do NOT beat yourself up or call yourself lazy if you can't wake up before dawn to write every day!

These exercises help you find nooks and crannies for writing, along with those coveted long swaths of time.

Exercise:

Open your calendar and pick your favorite color.

Go through the next year and use your favorite color to highlight spaces you could write. It could be weekly on your day off, monthly when you're doing long term planning, every other Thursday when your sister-in-law watches the kids, or during a quarterly mini writing retreat. Or maybe, like Glennon Doyle or Rachel Rodgers, you actually enjoy rising with the sun to pen your poetry while the house is quiet. No one knows your schedule and energy levels like you do, so comb through your calendar, ensuring that you still have time for self-care and rest, and see where there is legitimately time for writing. If you can carve out 15 minutes for some flash writing, highlight that time with your favorite color. If you have a 2 or 4 or 8 hour window, highlight it, too. Be realistic, but creative.

Exercise:

Now that you know when you can write, begin setting doable due dates throughout the year. You can do this in two ways (or both and find the average).

The first way is to decide when you want your manuscript finished and work BACK-WARDS, setting due dates on your calendar to meet your end goal.

For example, if it's October 1 and you want your manuscript finished by January 1, then you work backwards to realize you have 92 days to write, which means you need to write around 545 words each day in order to make your final due date.

The second option is to set due dates FORWARDS by seeing when you have time, how much you can write during that time, and setting due dates accordingly, noting when you'll reach your final word count as your completion date.

For example, if it's October 1 and you know you can write for about 4 hours each week, and on average you write roughly 500 words per hour, that's about 2,000 words per week. This means you'll need about 25 weeks to complete your manuscript, likely finishing around the end of March.

I recommend doing both the BACKWARDS and FORWARDS methods to discern what is most doable and reasonable for you.

With the above examples, if your FORWARDS due date tells you that you only have time to write roughly 2,000 words each week, but your BACKWARDS due date tells you that you really want to finish your manuscript by January 1, you'll need to create more time to write in October, November, and December by either adding more weekly writing time or setting aside a couple weekends or full days to do mini writing retreats. Or you have to adjust your expectations regarding when you can finish the manuscript.

My BACKWARDS due date is:

My FORWARDS due date is:

Book Writing Timeline Cheat Sheet
Daily and Weekly Word Counts

Before you complete this exercise, I've provided you with a helpful cheat sheet below that tells you exactly how much you need to write each day, week, and month in order to complete a manuscript in one month, three months, six months, nine months, and one year. Every writer has a personalized timeline for writing a book and every book is a slightly different length. However, it helps the writing process to know roughly how much you need to write daily, weekly, or monthly in order to complete a 50,000-word draft manuscript since this is the average length of a book. Below is a helpful guide, ranging from one month to one year. Add at least one month for beta readers and editing to each timeline so you can have a polished manuscript. Of course, if your book is research oriented, you must also allocate time for research.

Book in a Month:

Use #NaNoWriMo for inspiration.

Daily: 1,667ish words

Weekly: 11,600ish words

Monthly: 50,000ish words

Book in 3 Months:

Daily: 555ish words

Weekly: 3,900ish words

Monthly: 16,650ish words

Book in 6 Months:

Daily: 277ish words

Weekly: 1,945ish words

Monthly: 6,800ish words

Book in 9 Months:

Daily: 185ish words

Weekly: 1,296ish words

Monthly: 5,550ish words

Book in a Year:

Daily: 130ish words

Weekly: 960ish words

Monthly: 3,900ish words

Emboldened by the cheat sheet, combine your FORWARDS and BACKWARDS due dates to determine when you will finish your book manuscript, along with several doable due dates along the way.

I will finish my book manuscript by

My first doable due date is

Write down other doable due dates below:

My Doable Due Dates Are:

Bonus: If you want accountability, which increases your possibility of success, share your due dates with a writing buddy!

Now that you've determined WHY, WHAT, and WHEN you're writing, and you have both your outline and a set of doable due dates, you should meet at least ONE doable due date before moving on to chapter two: Book Diva Marketing.

Need some extra accountability, structure, and encouragement as you write your book?

Tehom Center Publishing offers 1:1 Book Doula coaching, in addition to multiple writing cohorts throughout the year. So, if you desire extra assistance as you write your manuscript, rest assured that Tehom Center Publishing has 1:1 and group coaching to help you succeed.

www.tehomcenter.org

Finally, in addition to meeting at least one doable due date before moving to the next chapter, make sure to stop and celebrate what you've achieved thus far. Marginalized writers need more joy, self-care, and celebration in our lives, so don't move on without acknowledging what you've accomplished thus far. Seriously, call or text a friend and brag about yourself. Pour your favorite cup of tea. Turn on your jam and shake your booty in celebration. Get a massage. Savor a long, luxurious stroll. Pick up some mouthwatering chocolate. Treat yourself. Whatever it might be, revel in the joy of completing the Book Doula portion of *The Authorpreneur Handbook*.

Exercise:

In the space below, write or draw how you're going to celebrate all you have accomplished in The Authorpreneur Handbook thus far. Then...celebrate!

Go you! You're amazing. Happy writing!

Book Diva Marketing

"The purpose of a writer is to make revolution irresistible."

— *Toni Cade Bombara*

CONGRATULATIONS ON MEETING your first doable due date! Remember to take a moment and CELEBRATE that achievement. You went from having a general idea of a book to discerning WHY you want to write it, WHAT you're going to write about, and WHEN you're going to complete the manuscript. That's a big deal.

Go you!

It's imperative that you keep writing and meeting your doable due dates while working through the rest of this handbook because a fabulous book marketing and authorpreneur plan are pretty useless without an actual book. So, keep writing as you read through this Book Diva Marketing chapter and complete the exercises.

The good news is that thinking creatively and strategically about book marketing will also benefit your writing, adding clarity and concision.

First, consider your relationship with the concept of marketing. It's not an area of expertise for most authors, or for many marginalized people. Traditional marketing, or what I often refer to as "bro marketing," is intentionally designed to trigger pain points to make us buy more stuff, stuff aimed at making us feel more "worthy" of the status quo. Because traditional marketing is grounded in white supremacist, patriarchal capitalism.

Boooo.

I'll be honest. Before truly living into my authorpreneur life, my relationship with marketing and money mindset was a wreck. When I thought about book marketing, or the concept of marketing in general, I immediately conjured a sleazy used car salesman with slicked back hair and oily palms, greased to sneakily steal money away from innocent people. I thought marketing was gross, antithetical to my intersectionally feminist and queer worldview.

I equated marketing with sales, and I didn't think sales could align with my values.

We do NOT want to do marketing like that. Rather, we want our marketing to align with our feminist, queer, antiracist values.

Exercise:

Take a moment to free write how you *feel* about marketing your book in the space below.

The Authorpreneur Handbook

Whether you think marketing is fabulous and become giddy at the thought of applying intersectional feminism to book marketing strategies or you break into hives at the thought of announcing your book on social media, keep reading because the exercises and information I'm sharing have taken many books to the #1 bestseller category and helped create the authorpreneur life writers dream of.

When I first began to realize that marketing didn't have to be sleazy, forsaking my values for the almighty dollar, I recall a dear friend sitting me down and explaining that I needed to decolonize my relationship with money.

Cross legged on a lava cliff overlooking the crashing Pacific on the Hawaiian island we both called home, she looked me squarely in the eyes and asked, "Does what you offer create transformative change?"

"Yes," I responded, tentatively.

"Has your work changed people's lives and made a difference in the world?"

"I believe so," I replied, this time slightly more confidently.

"Then how dare you keep that to yourself!" she insisted.

"Marketing is just sharing that transformation with others. Keeping it to yourself isn't just bad marketing, it's selfish."

Snap.

If Toni Cade Bombara is right in claiming that "the purpose of a writer is to make revolution irresistible," (and let's be real, of course she's right!) then how dare we keep our writing to ourselves. There is no revolution without marketing.

I'll say that again.

There is no revolution without marketing.

Marketing a book that offers transformational change is basically community organizing.

Given my background as an activist, a queer clergywoman, and person who spent much of her life below the poverty line, saying and believing this involves a lot of undoing, a lot of deconstructing the lies white supremacist cisheteropatriarchal capitalism told me, a lot of decolonizing my money mindset. But our writing cannot make revolution irresistible if no one reads our books. And no one will read our books if we do not effectively market them.

Return to your WHY for a moment. WHY are you writing this book in the first place?

Is it so you can have a dusty copy sitting on your shelf that no one else reads, the transformation within discovered only by a couple beta readers, an editor, and your publisher?

No.

Of course not.

You're writing a book to make a difference in the world. The only way to make that difference is for people to know about it. And to know about it, they have to buy it (or get it from the library) and read it! So, book marketing is simply spreading the good news of the transformation YOUR book is providing with the world.

It's not bragging.

It's not greedy.

It's not selfish.

It's healing. Transformational. Generous. Revolutionary.

In order to get the good news of your book out into the world, we have to subvert the systems already in place to our benefit. Even systems we may not like a lot. Even systems like Amazon.com.

[Insert ominous music]

Yes, Amazon.com…

The Power of 50 People: Creating Your Ultimate Launch Team

It's time to find your Micro Influencers.

50 is the magic number of Amazon reviews needed to boost the algorithm so that your book becomes a "recommended" purchase. So, 50 committed reviews on Amazon will automatically boost your sales and do the marketing for you.

All of our marketing, grounded in our aligned intersectionally feminist values, is aimed at the number 50.

Make a list of at least 50 people who would be willing to support your book and your work. Think of family, friends, and colleagues who already champion your work and would love to share your book with the world. If you struggle to make a list of 50, crowd source it on social media; you'd be surprised at who might volunteer! I once crowd sourced my launch team and a person I'd completely forgotten about volunteered. Who knew my chemistry partner from high school would have the slightest interest in supporting my book when we hadn't spoken in twenty years?

The point is that you never know who will come out of the woodwork to support your book if you don't ask. The goal of the list isn't fame or notoriety, though a few influencers on the list wouldn't hurt! Rather, the goal is DEDICATION. Who are the people who truly believe in you and your WHY and will commit to supporting you and your book?

Ask this list of people to do 3 simple things:

- Order and read your book (though you should provide them all with an Advance Reader Copy PDF during preorder)
- Commit to posting an honest review of your book on Amazon during launch week
- Commit to posting a link, image, and copy (all provided by you) on social media the week your book is published

Even if these 50 people only have a social media audience of 300 each, that's still 15,000 people who will learn about your book because they post about it. Maybe your great aunt Erma has a dedicated Facebook following of 327 people, but your niece's TikTok following of 83,000 reaches an even broader audience. Great Aunt Erma's faithful followers buy your book and call their local libraries to order it. Your niece Cayden inspires her TikTok followers to make up a dance with your book in their hands. And 48 other friends and colleagues review and post about your book on their myriad platforms.

Larona's Launch Team

Larona balked at the idea of asking fifty people to help market her book.

"I don't even know fifty people," she claimed.

Then she began brainstorming a list. First, she thought of other writers she knew. She was always willing to review their books, so they'd likely be willing to support her in return.

Her local writing group, a couple social media groups for women writers, and the small community of writers she met on a queer writing retreat came to mind. Wow, that's already 22 people on her list! Then she listed family and close friends who are always there when she needs them. Now her list has 32 people on it. Larona remembered her college roommate, which inspired a list of friends and colleagues from undergrad, grad school, and even back to high school. 44. Her work bestie decided to help her with the list, reminding her of all the organizations she's trained over the past year alone.

Larona leads Diversity, Equity, Inclusion, and Belonging (DEIB) trainings for nonprofits and corporations and her evaluations are always stellar. Her work bestie opened the database of organizations that went through Larona's training in the past year. There were 47, most of whom Larona is still in touch with personally and professionally. And that was just the points of contact at each organization. There were also quite a handful of people she met through these trainings who became trusted friends and colleagues, eager to support her work in myriad ways.

"That's just the list from this past year," her work bestie exclaimed. "Didn't that one nonprofit Executive Director from Oregon send you flowers on your birthday *and* a holiday gift? That training was three years ago!"

Larona and her work bestie revisited the files from the past three years, only adding people and organizations to her list if she had a true connection with them and their values aligned with the values of her book. By the time she finished, her launch team list was 316 people deep! Larona crafted a thoughtful email that included a simple two-minute survey for anyone interested in serving on her launch team.

She didn't get 50 people to agree.

Larona got 211 people on her launch team! She was blown away, but knew not everyone would fulfill their commitment because life is busy and people forget. But when her book was published, she faithfully emailed her launch team reminders and by the time her book was only 48 hours old, Larona had 186 Amazon reviews!

How's that for hacking the algorithm with the revolutionary power of community?

Maybe you don't train nearly 50 organizations annually like Larona, but you do have communities and people in your corner you may not usually think of.

Exercise:

Make this list of at least 50 people for your Launch Team in the space provided below.

My Ultimate Launch Team:

1.	11.
2.	12.
3.	13.
4.	14.
5.	15.
6.	16.
7.	17.
8.	18.
9.	19.
10.	20.

21.   36.

22.   37.

23.   38.

24.   39.

25.   40.

26.   41.

27.   42.

28.   43.

29.   44.

30.   45.

31.   46.

32.   47.

33.   48.

34.   49.

35.   50.

Combine your list of at least 50 people with crowd-sourced volunteers into one email group and share a simple survey inviting them to commit to particular elements of sharing your book with the world. The goal is for at least 50 people to commit to doing the 3 simple things listed above (reading, reviewing, posting). Some may be willing to go above and beyond with additional marketing ideas like:

- Posting about your book on social media a second time during the first year of your book's publication*
- Promoting your book on their email list, blog, or podcast
- Hosting or recommending your book in their book club
- Hosting a live or virtual book event
- Connecting you with an organization, school, or church that would use your book
- Connecting you with an influencer to promote your book
- Organizing and coordinating communication with your launch team
- Reaching out to local media about your book on your behalf
- Being your cheerleader. Publishing a book can be harrowing, lonely, and overwhelming, so you need some encouragers checking on your mental health from time to time.

*If everyone on your launch team posts on social media during launch week and all 50 people are also willing to post one more time on social media, you can divide the list so that each week of the entire year has someone posting about your book on social media.

Launch week + 50 weeks + 1 vacation week = 52 weeks (or one year of weekly book features on social media!)

Don't underestimate the importance of the mental health check-ins during your book launch. Writing and publishing a book can be incredibly isolating with a lot of triggering emotions popping up. Even if someone on your launch team has zero social media, no Amazon account, and knows nothing about book marketing, if that person is sincerely willing to consistently check on your wellbeing throughout the book launch process, you will have the launch team of your dreams.

Exercise:

Brainstorm a list of other ways you could ask your launch team to help promote your book in the space provided below.

Angela Yarber

The Power of 50 Pitches
Bianca's Body Positive Pitches

Bianca's book was four months from publication with possibilities for pre-order just around the corner, and she knew the power of companion essays for marketing. Rather than becoming overwhelmed or writing willy-nilly, she approached it strategically with a spreadsheet. While she had a goal of getting a few big splashy pieces published in places like the *New York Times*, *HuffPo*, or *Time Magazine*, Bianca also knew the power of niche media for connecting more specifically with her target audience.

Bianca's book fuses memoir with a how-to guide and she writes from the perspective of being a fat woman solo traveler, sharing both the joy and discrimination she faces as a fat woman flying, driving, and boating around the globe, while also providing practical tips for other fat women travelers. Clearly, Bianca can approach media and companion essays from a variety of angles. And with her handy spreadsheet, she divided the angles, essays, and outlets into categories and started pitching.

Bianca listed the major media outlets that were her big goals, in addition to major and niche travel magazines, blogs, podcasts, television, and radio shows. She also included a few big travel influencers on this list. But she didn't forget the power of smaller, more niche, and local media. She pitched her local news stations, local NPR in her hometown, alumni magazine from college, quite a few body positive and fat positive bloggers and podcasters, and a few airline magazines. If a chapter of her book touched on a particular city, country, or national park, Bianca reached out to their tourism boards and found out which blogs, websites, and local magazines might be interested in a location-specific essay from the perspective of a fat woman traveler.

Obvious angles for pitches included travel and solo women's travel, along with fat and body positivity. But Bianca didn't stop there. As a multiracial person who stands out as a foreigner in some settings, but blends into many that aren't necessarily part of her racial identity, she also wrote a couple companion pieces touching on race, even though it wasn't much of a theme in her book. And as a former choir director at a few churches, she tapped into a network of church newsletters because two chapters in her book discuss singing in churches around the world.

Thrilled to secure a splashy essay in *Forbes*, Bianca was also delighted to have so many church newsletters sharing her book, in addition to it trending across a variety of body positivity platforms, including email newsletters, blogs, and podcasts. Plus, she interviewed on a small, local news station when they had a summer segment on having a "beach body." All the other guest authors discussed workouts, diets, and swimsuits that mask "problem areas" of your body. Bianca stole the show as she passionately talked about her book, sharing stories of swimming in the Mediterranean, basking proudly in her fat body at nude beaches in Barcelona, or snorkeling in Thailand.

"Here's the key to having a beach body," she told the television host. "Have a body. Go to the beach!"

The audience was rapt. The segment did so well, it was picked up by the regional news station and then the state. What started as a tiny, local mid-morning 6-minute news segment where Bianca's book was one of many turned into several weeks of really fabulous marketing that led to more podcast interviews, a radio interview, a book feature in a regional magazine, and invitations to guest blog.

Audiences and readers ranged from a few hundred to hundreds of thousands, but because Bianca paced herself and had 50 different iterations of media coverage spread out over time, her book was in front of a variety of audiences every week for a solid year. Interestingly, when her publisher tracked her sales, she sold as many books when she had a major piece at a massive media outlet as she did when a dear friend featured her book with a guest newsletter piece to their email list of 3,300. Because those personal, niche audiences were *her* target readers. And all the companion essays, podcast interviews, and media highlights weren't only good book marketing, they also added more people to Bianca's email list and brought in more clients, thereby paving the way for her to live her dream authorpreneur life.

50 Media Outlets

One of the most impactful ways to market your book is through publishing companion essays. A Companion Essay is an essay that somehow relates to your book where you can casually link your book in both the body of the essay and in your author bio. For example, if your book deals with travel and you're a person with a disability, you might write a companion essay about this topic and say something like, "When writing my book, (link book here), I couldn't help but notice how inaccessible state parks were." Most publications don't want an essay *about* your book; they want a story that will engage their readers, but you can easily work your book into your essay naturally.

Think about what media outlets—newspapers, magazines, blogs, journals, podcasts, entrepreneur or activist newsletters, alumni magazines, church newsletters—that might publicize your book in some way, be it a book review, press release, or companion essay.

If you struggle to make a list of 50, reach out to your 50 people; some of them surely have podcasts, blogs, and connections to media outlets and they'd be happy to connect you!

Exercise:

Brainstorm a list of media outlets.

Think of big and splashy, smaller and more niche, and even seemingly quaint, like church or neighborhood newsletters.

50 Angles

Think of different angles you could take when writing companion essays about your book. Angles can include both identity and topic.

Identity.

What is your unique identity? For example, if you are a queer, black woman with ADHD, you could write from any of these identities as your starting point. You could also write from the perspective of any of these intersections of your identity.

Topic.

What are you writing about? If your book addresses eating disorders, white supremacy, and growing up as a latch key kid, these are all topics you can write about in a companion essay. Your WHAT includes myriad topic angles.

Coming up with 50 companion essays is incredibly daunting, but if you divide them into categories and apply your identity and topic angles to each category, making a list of 50 is easy peasy!

Here are 5 Companion Essay Categories:

1. Cutting Floor
2. Listicles
3. Why I Wrote this Book
4. Seasonal
5. News and Pop Culture

Cutting floor, pieces edited out of your book, direct book excerpts

These are parts of the book you edited out or excerpts from the book you publish as is. Make sure your publishing contract allows you to publish excerpts. At Tehom Center Publishing, for example, authors maintain 100% of the rights to their writing, so authors can publish as many excerpts as they'd like.

Listicles

Made famous by BuzzFeed, listicles are now lauded by Everyday Feminism, Psychology Today, and more. Think: "5 Ways to Honor Your Mental Health During the Holidays," "7 Ways to Celebrate Self-Care During Divisive Elections," or "6 Ways to Recover from Purity Culture."

Why I Wrote this Book (from different angles)

Smaller, niche publications will be interested in why you wrote your book, particularly from an angle that relates specifically to their niche. Think: an alumni magazine on why you wrote your book as a first-generation college student, Biology Major, student athlete or even a church newsletter on why you wrote your book as a queer Unitarian Universalist.

Tie into seasonal (Women's History Month, Pride, holidays, etc)

Tying your essay into something seasonal makes it more likely for an editor to pick it up. For example, if you are queer or your book has any queer themes, Pride is a great time to pitch companion essays.

Tie into the news cycle (elections, pop culture, etc)

Tying your essay into a current event is the most likely for an editor to pick it up. Though the example is enraging, there are always stories in the news cycle about a famous person sexually assaulting someone; if your book grapples with sexual assault in any way, having an essay at the ready to pitch when it's relevant in the news cycle is invaluable.

Exercise:

Brainstorm a list of essays for each of the 5 categories listed above. Remember to use both identity and topic as angles.

Excerpts and Cut Pieces

1.

2.

3.

4.

5.

6.

7.

8.

9.

10.

Listicles

1.

2.

3.

4.

5.

6.

7.

8.

9.

10.

Why I Wrote this Book

1.

2.

3.

4.

5.

6.

7.

8.

9.

10.

Seasonal

1.

2.

3.

4.

5.

6.

7.

8.

9.

10.

News Cycle

1.

2.

3.

4.

5.

6.

7.

8.

9.

10.

HOW to pitch:

Always follow the exact guidelines for how to pitch an essay that a publication provides, but use the framework below as a helpful starting point.

If you want to learn more about successfully pitching essays, I recommend Susan Shapiro's *Byline Bible*.

> *Dear [Editor Name],*
>
> *I'm writing to submit an essay on [insert hook of book or essay]. I truly enjoyed your recent piece about [insert recent piece] because [insert why it resonated]. My [insert word count] essay grapples with [2-3 sentences max] and it would be a good fit for [your magazine] because [brief reason that ties to mission].*
> *I am an author of [book and name of 1-2 good bylines with embedded links] with expertise in [insert relevant expertise] and I would be delighted to write for [magazine].*
>
> *Sincerely,*
> *[Name, email, phone number]*

Exercise:

Write your first pitch! Decide where you want to pitch your first companion essay and look up the submission guidelines. Combining their specific guidelines with the framework above, write your first pitch. Proofread it. Then actually send it! Seriously. Don't move on to the next section until you've written and sent your pitch!

(Hint: If you're having trouble finding the precise editor for your pitch, locate the masthead on the outlet's website and submit accordingly.)

The Authorpreneur Handbook

My First Pitch:

50 Possibilities: Programs, Dreams, and Fun Extras

In addition to the 50 people who are going to help launch your book and the 50 media outlets who will feature it, marketing can also include an array of fun possibilities.

50 possibilities, in fact.

Overwhelming, I know. But I'm here to help you through the overwhelm with—you guessed it—another division of list ideas!

Think of at least 50 possibilities related to marketing your book. Divide these possibilities into 5 different categories with 10 items on each of the 5 lists.

1. Events
2. Virtual Goodies
3. Giveaways
4. Fun Extras
5. Collaborations

1. Events:

Plan events aimed at marketing your book, including, but not limited to:

- book signings
- book tour
- lectures
- Zoom gatherings
- Facebook or Instagram Live
- book launch party
- yoga/book combo
- book/music combo
- book/gallery combo
- book/food combo
- collaboration events

Kalinda's book dreams of constellating life by centering queerness. Though the book is not technically about space or constellations, they partner with the planetarium for an

Evening of Reading Under the Stars where they sign books, share a reading aloud, guide participants in an exercise on how to constellate their life, and have cozy nooks for quiet reading throughout the space.

Keisha is a yoga teacher and wrote a book about yoga and breathwork as a part of sex therapy. For the first month after her book is published, she incorporates brief readings at the end of each yoga class she teaches during final shavasana and hosts a handful of Books and Yoga Events with local yoga studios.

Kat's book is about Diversity, Equity, Inclusion, and Belonging (DEIB) work in elementary schools, but they also have a background as a voice actor. Kat does a weekly Instagram Live where they read serious portions of their book in different accents and ridiculously silly voices; the humor helps soften the seriousness of their message and the Lives go viral with thousands of people tuning in, buying their book, and becoming aware of their powerful work.

Exercise:

Make a list of at least 10 different event ideas for marketing your book. (Hint: you can offer the same event in 10 different locations, too!)

Book Event Ideas:

1.

2.

3.

4.

5.

6.

7.

8.

9.

10.

2. Virtual goodies:

Who doesn't love virtual goodies that go along with a book and enhance the book's mission? Ideas include, but are not limited to:

- Playlist inspired by the book
- #hashtag photo challenges for readers
- social media contests
- reels series
- social media graphics
- downloadable PDF related to your book's WHY (hint: this is a great way to grow your email list, too, and functions as a lead magnet for your work!)
- Youtube videos
- TikTok videos

Lakshmi wrote a stunning cookbook that includes recipes, gorgeous photos of her food against jaw-dropping landscapes, and stories of cooking with her grandmother when she lived in India as a child. Her book ignites the senses with taste, smell, texture, and visual stimulation, but she wants readers to experience the fullness of the senses, so she put together a Spotify playlist for readers to listen to for each recipe and chapter. Plus, she created a social media challenge where readers shared the songs they listened to while cooking her recipes; this increased her visibility and book marketing tremendously.

Laura's queer romance novel included a photo of her toes in the sand at the beach with her toenails painted neon purple on the cover. She used this as a marketing tool by creating a hashtag with her book's title and the word "toes" and readers posted photos of themselves reading her book with their toes peeking out all over socials. Some even painted their toes to match! Laura even created a contest for readers to vote on the most creative toe pics. This increased engagement and marketed her book to a wider audience, with it trending among nail techs who would have never otherwise known about her book.

Lee is a wiz with graphic design and has a keen eye for making snappy graphics on Canva. They asked their publisher for the color and font codes from their book cover and whipped together 3 different designs that amplified the aesthetic and brand of their book. In one hour, Lee cut and pasted quotes from their book, reviews, and endorsements. By the end of the hour, Lee had over 30 pieces of original content related to their book and scheduled them to post on socials, thereby having long-term social media marketing, a shareable media kit for their launch team, and a consistent brand aesthetic that all pointed back to their book.

Exercise: *Make a list of at least 10 different virtual goodies ideas for marketing your book.*

Virtual Goodies Ideas:

1.

2.

3.

4.

5.

6.

7.

8.

9.

10.

3. Giveaways:

You may be thinking, "Why on earth should I *give* something away to help market my book?" Perhaps you've heard the cliché, "You've got to spend money to make money." Well, that rings true here. Plus, not all giveaways need to cost money! Everyone loves free stuff and giving away something special to your readers, people who pre-order, or special fans helps honor their commitment to your work and thank them for their support.

Consider giveaway ideas like:

- Drawings for a free copy of your book on social media, Goodreads, and at book events
- Raffles
- Bookmarks with your book cover on them and a QR code to order more
- Postcards that align with your book aesthetic with a handwritten note
- Book Club Q&A Guide
- Art Print with an inspirational quote from your book
- Free "Ask the Author" session

Teresa wrote a beautiful book about contemplative creativity for marginalized people. She's also a very talented artist. Her artwork shined on the cover of her book and readers seemed to love the art just as much as the book itself. So, she created small art prints featuring the art from the book cover and included a QR code on the back to order the book. She gave everyone who pre-ordered her book a free art print, in addition to providing stacks at local galleries and coffee shops that hosted book events. This led both to more book sales and to making readers feel special. Teresa printed in a low-cost manner by simply making color copies on cardstock at an office supply store, thereby only spending about 0.38 cents per image. Bonus: so many people liked Teresa's mini prints that there was enough demand for a limited-edition larger print run that she sold for $75 per 11x14 print!

Tamika's launch team had at least 8 different book club leaders in it. Plus, Tamika had been a part of several book clubs in the past, and one of her dear friends and launch team members was part of a book club training program that connected people with online book clubs based on genre and interest. Tamika made a book club packet for anyone who used her book in their book club. Her packet was free, downloadable on her website, and included a list of discussion questions, themed snacks inspired by her book, a recipe for a book-themed cocktail or mocktail, an icebreaker game based on one of her chapters, and even some fun décor ideas for those who wanted their book club to go the extra mile. Book clubbers *loved* it and responded by taking a lot of photos and sharing them on socials with links to buy the book.

Terika decided to make her readers work a little for her free giveaway. With a book rooted in Alice Walker's womanist notion of "loving your body, regardless," she hosted a body positivity challenge for her readers on social media. Everyone who posted a photo of themselves holding her book with a caption affirming their body won a free downloadable PDF filled with body affirmations. Plus, at the end of the contest, everyone voted on a winner and the winner received a free body positivity coaching session with Terika. Not only did this challenge and giveaway help with book marketing, but it also ended up forming a community of sisterhood where participants encouraged one another. This alone was positive. Plus, Terika saw a need and leveraged the positivity and community support into a low-cost, high-impact membership program where she offers group body positivity coaching.

Exercise:

Make a list of at least 10 different giveaway ideas for marketing your book.

Giveaway Ideas:

1.

2.

3.

4.

5.

6.

7.

8.

9.

10.

4. Fun Extras:

Fun extras are the things that may not always have a direct impact on book marketing, but elevate the book, reader, and author experience in the world in ways that are delightful, engaging, and fun. Most of the ideas do have at least an indirect impact on book marketing.

Some fun extras book ideas include, but are not limited to:

- print book covers on earrings or a pendant (hint: lots of Etsy artists offer this)
- print your book cover on a cake
- make or commission themed cookies
- create a signature book-themed cocktail or tea blend
- create a fun book coloring page
- order a book t-shirt with a snazzy quote or image from the book (hint: use a print-on-demand platform so as to not incur any upfront costs)
- book tote bags
- book Selfie-Sign or Selfie-Station for book events

Maya had a lot of in-person book events, in addition to going on a book tour, and she wanted each event to be uniquely special, while also having a uniting element. So, Maya spent about $100 designing a big Selfie-Sign and buying a few fun props that correlated with her book. The color purple was a motif in her book, so she had purple hats, a purple feather boa, and purple signs with a catch phrase one of her characters used a lot in her novel. She used all of this to create a fun, interactive Selfie Station at all her events. Not only were her in-person events joyful and engaging, but most of the attendees took a lot of photos and posted them enthusiastically on social media. With the QR to order her book front and center on the giant Selfie-Sign in every single photo, even more people eagerly ordered her book.

Max adores wearing giant earrings almost as much as they love writing. When they saw that different jewelry designers can print book earrings featuring their book cover, Max jumped on the idea, thinking it would simply be a fun accessory that made them feel proud while looking fierce. Almost every time Max rocks the earrings, they get compliments and questions about them, often leading the person to order the book on their smartphone right away!

Miss Queen of D-Nile is a drag queen quite famous in her region and she published a book of drag queen affirmations accompanying glamorous, campy photos of herself. To celebrate her book launch, she found an app that converted images into coloring pages. Selecting three images with affirmations, Miss Queen spent roughly $30 printing a bunch of coloring pages that included the book order QR code in the corner, along with a link to her website. Every time she did a drag show, Drag Story Time, drag bingo, or book event, she'd hand out free coloring pages. Children and adults alike colored the pages and posted images on social media using the hashtag Miss Queen recommended. Her reach quickly extended outside her region until drag queens across the country were passing out her free coloring pages at events, driving even more people to order her book and join her following.

Exercise:

Make a list of at least 10 different fun extras ideas for marketing your book.

Fun Extras Ideas:

1.

2.

3.

4.

. . .

5.

6.

7.

8.

9.

10.

5. Collaborations:

Juanita is a queer poet and activist who just published a chapbook. She goes to a queer-owned salon and barber shop that has a small event space where they sometimes host activities for the LGBTQ community. Juanita has known her stylist for nearly a decade and they often joke about which one of them is more excited about Juanita's book coming out. Together, they decide to host a Queer Poetry and Pampering Night at the salon. Juanita will sell her book, read a few of her poems, and organize a poetry sharing time, while her stylist is offering free flash face massages, discounted blow outs, and free hair consultations. Juanita's book reaches a new audience, her stylist's salon gets new clients, and both support the queer community with radical self-care for collective liberation. Win win.

Joy is both a first-generation immigrant and first-generation college student who wrote a thriller that touches on these themes. Jaya is also first gen, but from a different country, and he wrote a how-to guide about starting a business while still in school. Like Joy and Jaya, Jarena is also first generation, but she wrote a memoir specifically about her experience. Though their genres are all completely different, Joy, Jaya, and Jarena share overlapping identities and WHYs. They collaborate to tour college campuses, focusing particularly on reaching international and first-generation students, sharing their stories, along with tools for navigating their overlapping experiences. At each event, not only do they sell books, but many schools add some of their books to required and recommended reading lists. Win win.

For over twenty years, Jamie oversaw joint venture marketing opportunities for a Fortune 500 company. Burned out by the 9-5 rat race, Jamie decided to leave corporate America to become an author, applying their marketing savvy to their debut novel about a park ranger whose disabilities became superpowers. Jamie reached out to every single organization and person they'd ever worked with who had a focus in the literary world, disability rights activism, or national parks. The list was nearly 200 deep! Jamie created a simple and effective media kit with graphics, the book cover, blurbs about the novel in a variety of lengths, social media content, and a brief, compelling newsletter article. Over 100 people or organizations agreed to collaborate with Jamie, sending their book information out to their audiences, while Jamie traded doing the same for their audience. Jamie's audience relished all the fascinating information, resources, discounts, and programs offered by their joint venture partners, and Jamie's book information reached hundreds of thousands of potential readers. The partners and partner organizations got new clients from Jamie's audience and Jamie got a lot of new readers. Win win.

A big part of feminist and queer marketing is collaboration rather than competition. When we help other marginalized people shine, we shine, too. When we offer our network and audience to people who share our values, their audience also becomes aware of us. Then all our audiences and networks grow. We all learn more. Our burdens are shared, and therefore, lightened. And the perspectives of the marginalized slowly inch closer to the center.

In Spanish, we call this *comadres en la lucha,* co-mothers in the struggle.

The same is true for your book marketing. Who are other authors, organizations, entrepreneurs, nonprofits, and people who align with your WHY? How can you and your book elevate their message? How can they elevate your book? How can you work *together* to elevate a mutual WHY?

Your ten possibilities can include people and organizations to collaborate with in addition to *how* you'll collaborate with them.

Bonus Hint: Remember your identity and topic angles for pitches? Invite your identity and topic to help you brainstorm types of people and organizations you could collaborate with for book marketing.

Exercise:

Brainstorm a list of at least 10 different collaboration partners. Include how you'd like to collaborate with the partner, as well (joint venture, live event, social media swap, Zoom event, tour events, etc.)

Collaboration Ideas:

1.

2.

3.

4.

5.

6.

7.

8.

9.

10.

Excuse me? Did you realize that you just made a list of 50 possibilities of marketing fabulousness for your forthcoming book?

That's a big deal!

Here's one more bonus thing you can do to make these possibilities even more likely to become reality. Flip back to the list of 50 people you made for your launch team. Think about some of their gifts, strengths, and networks and see where they might be able to lend a helping hand with some of your 50 possibilities. Maybe you have a dream event planner on your team or someone who doesn't mind making phone calls or a launch team member who owns a bookstore or winery or bakery or really loves to find weird deals on random things on the internet (like book stickers, bookmarks, Selfie Signs, etc). If so, they'd probably be willing to help you with some of the items on your 50 Possibilities List. So, read back through your 50 Possibilities Lists and make a note of any item on the list that a particular person on your launch team might be able to help make happen.

Now, let's make these possibilities a reality!

Exercise:

It's time to implement some of these exercises. Before moving to Chapter 3—Book Dream-Maker Authorpreneur—be sure to complete at least 5 items from your To-Do Marketing list. Your To-Do Marketing List involves taking an action step toward at least one item from each section of your 50 Possibilities Lists: 1) Events, 2) Virtual Goodies, 3) Giveaways, 4) Fun Extras, 5) Collaborations.

You don't actually have to *do* the thing yet, but you do need to take an action step toward making one thing from each of the five lists happen. For example, if you want to have a book event at your local library, contact the library to request information. If you want themed graphics that match your book's cover design, hop on Canva and experiment with design. If you want to give away free bookmarks, research companies that sell bookmarks. You get the idea. Take five steps in the direction of making your 50 possibilities realities.

My To-Do Marketing List:

1.

2.

3.

4.

5.

Congratulations! Not only are you writing your book and meeting doable due dates, but you've also completed all the exercises necessary for formulating a strategic book marketing plan that aligns with your values.

Do a happy dance!

Combined, your 50 people, 50 pitches, and 50 possibilities, implemented over a period of 50 weeks (plus launch week and a week of vacation, which you totally deserve) gives you an official one-year book marketing plan! You are now prepared to share your transformational message with the world!

You're so close, but you're not quite done with planning your book marketing yet!

Nope.

It's time to get your calendar back out and grab your favorite color highlighter (IRL or virtual). Remember all those doable due dates on your writing calendar? Well, it's time to apply that same methodology to your marketing. All these lists are great, but without doable due dates affixed to them, you simply have a lot of notes on a page of a book. So, return to your final doable due date—your publication date—and begin creating your one-year book marketing plan!

When will you invite potential launch team members, survey your launch team, write and pitch those companion essays, schedule those book events, or order that fabulously delicious book cover cake? All those items on your lists deserve dates. This far in advance, it may be tough to decide *exact* dates for every single thing, but you can assign tasks to particular weeks and months. For example, if you're planning an epic book launch party at a fancy location that requires advanced reservations, you probably want to narrow down a particular date for that. But if you want to pitch a companion essay to coincide with the holiday season, you can simply set a due date of early November to have the essay and pitch completed.

Planning your one-year book marketing strategy with your calendar in hand also helps you be aware of the seasons in your life and other work. If you're a sports reporter, for example, you probably don't want to schedule a massive launch party on opening day. If you're clergy, it's likely you don't want your book tour kicking off in the middle of Holy Week. If you're a parent, planning big book events around your kiddo's birthday may not be the wisest. If there's an anniversary or season that's particularly difficult for your mental health, it's probably not the best time to go on a podcast tour. So, be mindful of the fullness of your life. Give yourself space to rest, breathe, and celebrate. Create a book marketing schedule that fills you with joy. And remember those beloved 50+ on your launch team and ask them for help.

Exercise:

Organize your one-year book marketing plan on your calendar with each listed item given a doable due date. Create a yearlong highlight reel in the space below, with doable due dates for each month following your projected publication date.

My One-Year Book Marketing Plan:

Month 1 (publication month) :

Month 2:

Month 3:

. . .

Month 4:

Month 5:

Month 6:

Month 7:

Month 8:

Month 9:

Month 10:

Month 11:

Month 12:

If you're feeling a bit overwhelmed or need some additional guidance and support in crafting and implementing your book marketing plan beyond this workbook, Tehom Center Publishing has equitable programs to help. We offer both 1:1 Book Diva Marketing Coaching and group cohorts that include the Book Diva Marketing program aimed at empowering authors in creating the ultimate one-year book marketing strategy, along with making vital connections in the industry to magazine editors, podcast hosts, book bloggers, social media influencers, and more.

You don't have to do this alone! Tehom Center Publishing has a community and network of support to help you every step of the way.

www.tehomcenter.org

Seriously. You just created a one-year book marketing plan with doable due dates and everything!

Take a deep breath.

Give yourself a pat on the back.

Now take a moment to flip back through the entire Book Diva marketing chapter of this handbook. Make a mental note of the exercises that excited you and the ones you found particularly challenging. What strokes of genius did you have? Where are you most proud? What item on your myriad lists ignites your imagination with creative potential?

Finally, in addition to making your one-year marketing plan and checking those five To-Do Marketing List items off your list before moving to the next chapter, make sure to stop and celebrate what you've achieved thus far. Marginalized writers deserve more joy, self-care, and celebration in our lives, so don't move on without acknowledging what you've accomplished. Seriously, call or text a family member and brag about yourself. Pour some coffee in your favorite mug. Watch a few minutes of reels featuring cute cuddly animals. Get your nails done. Take a long, luxurious bath. Pick up some mouth-watering pastries. Treat yourself. Whatever it might be, revel in the joy of completing the Book Diva portion of *The Authorpreneur Handbook*.

Exercise:

In the space below, write or draw how you're going to celebrate all you have accomplished in The Authorpreneur Handbook thus far. Then...celebrate!

I told you you're capable of intersectionally feminist and fun marketing! You're fabulous. Happy marketing!

Book DreamMaker Authorpreneur

"One person plus one typewriter constitutes a movement."

— *Pauli Murray*

Pauli Murray knew what it meant to start a movement.

Murray was a queer, black woman raised in Durham, NC by her aunt after her parents died. She was a civil rights attorney, coining the phrase "Jane Crow" to acknowledge the role of sexism in addition to racism in Jim Crow laws. In her sixties, she became the first African American woman to be ordained as an Episcopal priest.

All the while she loved women, even claiming that if she could transition from Pauli to Paul, she would, thus providing hope, not only for women, lesbians, and African Americans, but also for transgender people.

Murray was ahead of her time in so many prophetic ways. She graduated from Hunter College, intent on attending law school so that she could work for justice for black women. In 1938, she was rejected from UNC Chapel Hill's law school because of her race and Harvard because of her gender. She even received a prestigious scholarship from Harvard when the admissions committee assumed that "Pauli" was a man's nickname;

upon discovering that Pauli was a woman, they revoked the scholarship and admission into the law school. Undeterred, she enrolled in law school at UC Berkeley.

Upon finishing, she published a book, *States' Laws on Race and Color*, which was described by Thurgood Marshall as the bible for civil rights attorneys. She lost a teaching post at Cornell University because of the people who wrote her references—the legendary Eleanor Roosevelt, Thurgood Marshall, and Philip Randolph—who were dubbed "too radical" by the university.

Yet Murray continued working for equality, jailed for organizing desegregation on public transportation years before Rosa Parks, in addition to planning sit-ins twenty years before the famous Woolworth's protests in Greensboro. In 1965, she was the first black woman to earn a law doctorate at Yale. As a celebration, she co-founded the National Organization for Women (NOW).

After challenging the status quo in law, Murray decided to pursue the priesthood in her sixties. She began her studies at New York's General Theological Seminary before the Episcopal Church permitted women to become priests. In 1977, she was ordained and presided at her first Eucharist (the Episcopalian word for communion, or the bread and wine that symbolize the body of Jesus) at the Chapel of the Holy Cross in Chapel Hill, NC. It was the same church where her grandmother—then enslaved—was baptized.

Throughout her career in civil rights and in the priesthood, Murray had loving, committed, and intimate relationships with women and struggled with her gender identity. Throughout the 20s and 30s she took hormone treatments as she described herself as a "man trapped in a woman's body."

Today Murray may have described herself as transgender or gender queer, though such language was not readily available to her during her lifetime. She lived and loved boldly, finding the magnanimous balance between humility and pride, and working tirelessly so that all may be treated equally.

Murray is remembered for claiming, "One person, plus one typewriter constitutes a movement."

And you may be thinking, "That's a cool story, Dr. Ang, and Pauli Murray definitely sounds like a badass revolutionary, but what on earth does Murray have to do with *my* authorpreneur life?"

I'll tell ya.

Living the authorpreneur life and accessing the financial abundance it can provide matters little without that deep, abiding WHY from chapter one guiding you. If your writing isn't constituting a movement for justice, equality, joy, or a better world, what's the point?

Being an authorpreneur is as much about accessing the wealth denied historically marginalized people as it is about constituting a movement. That's what Murray's work was all about. Further, one of Murray's gripping poems in the book of the same name, *Dark Testament*, beckons us:

> *Hope is a song in a weary throat*
> *Give me a song of hope*
> *And a world where I can sing it.*
> *Give me a song of faith*
> *And a people to believe in it.*
> *Give me a song of kindliness*
> *And a country where I can live it.*
> *Give me a song of hope and love*
> *And a brown girl's heart to hear it.*

Given all that Murray suffered, she still dared to hope, to dream. Her words and poetry are reminders that living the authorpreneur life is grounded in hope and dedicated to movement building. It's about providing ourselves, as marginalized writers, and our readers with a song of hope.

As we begin this chapter on Authorpreneurship, Book DreamMaking, and all the money involved in making those dreams a reality, I don't want us to forsake the song of hope or the movement our writing must constitute. Remember this when you feel bogged down by conversations about money mindset and finances in this chapter.

You're working on writing your book and you've dedicated time to creating a strategic book marketing plan filled with 50 people, 50 pitches, and 50 possibilities. That is amazing! You are well on your way to living the authorpreneur life of your dreams.

Being an authorpreneur doesn't stop with writing, publishing, and marketing your book, though. To become an authorpreneur, you need to learn to leverage your book to build your business and brand. And that's what this chapter of *The Authorpreneur Handbook* does. Before we talk about funding your dream author life by creating a book funnel and flywheel, let's figure out exactly what your dream life is!

Can you imagine it? Picture yourself one year down the road. You've written and published your book and you're living the authorpreneur life of your dreams. What does that life look, taste, feel, smell, and sound like? What emotions does it stir in you?

Exercise:

Take 10 minutes to free write, answering the question, "What does my dream writer life look like?"

Get detailed. If you want to write for 3 hours a day, take a nap, have a private chef, and enjoy a long stroll around your neighborhood, write it down. If you want to pay off debt and empower queer kids with your writing, include it in your dream life. If writing poetry on a vintage typewriter in the middle of a mossy forest is your jam, own it by jotting it down.

Now take a deep breath.

Inhale the hope and movement and dream life you're imagining.

Let the breath of it fill your lungs and body.

Exhale any limiting beliefs preventing you from living fully into your dream authorpreneur life.

Now, let's figure out how to make this dream life a reality.

For me, the magic occurs when we combine dreams with strategy.

I imagine your dream authorpreneur life isn't free, is it? Living your dream life requires money and my guess is that you probably don't want to work an additional job to fund your dream writer life, so let's dive into some money strategies to help make this dream writer life possible.

Money Mindset.

When you think of money and creating a business funnel related to your book, what immediately pops into your mind? What is your mindset surrounding money?

Exercise:

Free write for five minutes regarding your own money mindset and financial hangups in the space provided below.

Whether you bask in financial abundance and have a healthy money mindset, rage against white supremacist patriarchal capitalism, or have lived your entire life (likely through absolutely no fault of your own) under the poverty line, addressing your relationship with money is an imperative way to begin thinking about living the authorpreneur life of your dreams.

Here's the thing. Marginalized people haven't had as many opportunities to create wealth as others. That's simply the way the system is designed. If you are BIPOC, queer, a woman, or a person with disabilities, actualizing financial abundance is harder. Full stop.

But it doesn't have to be this way.

Living the authorpreneur life is about subverting these broken systems so that marginalized people have access to abundance. That includes YOU. Because when marginalized people thrive, we all thrive. I invite you to dispel some money myths and claim abundance for the global good.

Exercise:

Take 15 minutes to peruse helloseven.co

This is not my organization and I'm not getting any kickbacks for sending you there. But Rachel Rodgers at Hello 7 is the boss at articulating WHY people at the margins deserve financial abundance...and how we can make it possible.

Jot down a few key takeaways from this perusal:

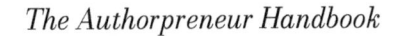

Bonus: Read *We Should All Be Millionaires* by Rachel Rodgers

Now that you're aligning your money mindset with your values, let's start talking about paid programming that aligns with the WHY and WHAT of your book. Think about what kind of paid programming you can offer where your book functions as a lead magnet for clients. A lead magnet is a low cost or free offering—your $25ish book, for example—that introduces people to who you are and what you offer the world. Lead magnets help people get to know and trust you; hopefully, the lead magnet drives someone to want to work with you because they experience how transformational your work is.

Angela Yarber

Penelope's Programs

Penelope always knew her voice was meant to be heard, but for years, her stories of survival and resilience as a queer woman of color remained locked inside her heart. Penelope had navigated trauma, healing, and self-discovery in ways that shaped her identity and her spirituality. Her journey led her to write a book about healing, transformation, and authenticity from the margins, a deeply personal reflection on her own experiences with trauma-informed care and spiritual recovery.

Her book sold modestly, resonating with readers who felt seen in her words. But Penelope knew the message of her book was bigger than the pages it was printed on—it was a tool that could spark transformation in others, just as it had for her. Her book was the start of a movement. She began to wonder how she could reach a larger audience and build a sustainable income, all while living authentically.

The idea struck her during a spiritual retreat: her book could serve as a lead magnet, introducing people to her work and inviting them into deeper transformation. The book would become a gateway, not the final destination.

Penelope launched a series of paid programs, offering workshops, retreats, and group coaching centered around the themes of the book. She knew the value of having an accessible entry point, with her book at a reasonable $25, marketing it as a low-cost investment in self-exploration. Readers who were drawn to her story would get a taste of her healing work, and from there, many were inspired to take the next step: joining her paid program.

Her first offering was a six-week online course that expanded on the practices in her book. It guided participants through trauma recovery, spiritual practices, and reclaiming their sense of self. The course filled quickly, drawing in a diverse group of participants who resonated with her story. The community she built was healing in itself—a space where queer people of color and others from marginalized backgrounds could be seen, heard, and supported.

But Penelope didn't stop there. She created additional workshops and trainings, each one building on the foundational work of her book. These offerings varied in price, allowing people at different stages of their healing journey to access her work. Some joined her for one-on-one coaching, while others attended her signature weekend retreats, where they could experience healing in person through group ceremonies and spiritual practices she developed.

As her community grew, so did her business. Penelope's paid programming became the backbone of her income, allowing her to leave her traditional job and focus fully on her passion. She crafted a life where her work and her spirit were fully aligned. Her book had done more than tell her story; it had transformed her into an authorpreneur, using her voice to not only create impact but also generate a sustainable business.

Through her book, Penelope had opened a door, but through her paid programs, she invited people to walk through it with her—and to find their own healing, light, and authenticity along the way. She had turned her experiences of marginalization into empowerment and became a beacon for others to do the same.

Penelope is now living the life she had always dreamed of—an authorpreneur who wasn't just selling books, but creating lasting, transformational change.

Paid Programming:
Aligning Paid Programs with Your Book's WHY and WHAT.

Inspired by Penelope, consider what kinds of paid programs align with the WHY and WHAT of your book.

Examples could include:

- Workshops
- Courses
- Trainings
- Memberships
- Signature speaking (or sermons)
- Retreats
- 1:1 coaching
- Group coaching
- Products
- Services
- Rituals

Exercise:

Brainstorm a list of program ideas that align with your book.

Now that you've brainstormed a list of possible programming that aligns with the WHY and WHAT of your book, begin to strategize pricing for each offering.

Creating a Funnel or Flywheel

The goal is to create 3+ signature programs that increase in depth and price to connect readers/clients more fully with the WHAT and WHY behind your book. This is also an equitable approach because you offer your transformations with free content and as low as $25ish so that it's accessible to anyone, no matter their means. But you also offer more depth and breadth for those who have the resources to pursue your wisdom and transformation further.

To begin, one offering should be around $25ish (this is your book), one offering around the $300ish range, one in the $1,500-$3,000ish, and bonus for one BIG ticket item that's around $10,000

For example, here is a funnel:

- Funnel Entry: FREE Lead Magnet
- $25ish: YOUR BOOK!
- $297 Course
- $2,500 Group Coaching
- $10,000 Luxurious Private Retreat

The funnel functions to welcome readers/clients into the revolutionary world of your work. They experience transformation and want to dive deeper, so they move into the narrower parts of the funnel with more enriching offers.

But don't let them leave, even after a big-ticket item!

Flywheel:

Create a constant, low-cost or free offering that maintains community and keeps readers/clients involved and wanting more.

Examples include:

- Membership Program
- Facebook Group
- Newsletter
- Coaching
- Monthly Zoom "Office Hours"
- Social Media Content
- Slack or Discord Channel

To give you a glimpse at actual numbers, let's check out Sonia's funnel and flywheel.

Sonia wrote a book about overcoming generational trauma through mindfulness meditation and, as a Cuban American, Sonia focuses on helping BIPOC women, and specifically Latinas.

Her book costs $25 and she receives 20% royalties. In one year, she sold 3,500 copies of her book. So, her book made $17,500 in one year. Sonia is proud of her book sales—as she should be—but she knows $17,500 is a drop in the bucket for what she needs to make a living.

Sonia also created a funnel and flywheel to help build her client list that looks like this:

Funnel Entry: FREE lead magnet
Sonia's free lead magnet is an online quiz that helps BIPOC women discern which meditation style is best for them. Everyone who takes the online quiz is automatically added to Sonia's email list. She has almost 2,000 people on her email list.

$25 BOOK!
Sonia sold 3,500 copies of her book in year one, making $17,500.

$297 Course
Sonia turned her book into a curriculum and filmed short videos with corresponding worksheets to help learners work through generational trauma with mindfulness techniques. She set up the course as an online, on demand, self-paced course that is always available on her website.

In one year, Sonia had 34 learners register for her course, making $10,098.

$2,500 One-on-One Coaching
The Call to Action at the end of Sonia's course invites learners to become 1:1 coaching clients with her. She offers a package of 8 sessions for $2,500 and had 18 clients in her first year, making $45,000.

$10,000 Luxurious Private Retreat
Sonia decided to take a risk and offer one big-ticket item, which is a luxury 5-day 1:1 retreat where Sonia gives her client 100% of her time, leading mindfulness meditation and coaching them through trauma work. Sonia lives in a beautiful travel destination and has a spare bedroom and bathroom, so she transformed it into an inspiring, soothing room to minimize overhead costs. She splurged on partnering with a private chef with shared values, so her financial investment in each private retreat is only $1,000. So, she profits $9,000 per retreat.

Sonia led 4 private retreats in the first year after her book launched, making $36,000.

Flywheel: $47 monthly membership
Sonia wanted to keep clients involved, so she created a monthly mindful meditation membership program for BIPOC women. Members meet every week for a group mindfulness session, in addition to receiving weekly mindfulness emails and being part of a private social media group where Sonia shares daily mindfulness prompts. She currently has 20 members paying $47 monthly, making $940 per month, or $11,280 annually.

Due to publishing her transformational book and developing a solid funnel with a flywheel, Sonia celebrates her one year book anniversary by earning $119,878!

Oh, and how could we forget that she was invited to give a keynote speech about Mindfulness that paid her a $5,000 honorarium, in addition to providing an all-expense paid trip to San Diego where the conference was hosted. And three smaller organizations hired her to lead mindfulness workshops, each paying her $1,500 for a 2-hour workshop.

Not only did she earn $9,500 from speaking engagements/workshops, but a fortune 100 CEO was a board member in one of her smaller workshops and invited her to speak at a corporate event on her same topic, confident that her mindfulness work would improve workplace productivity. This speaking gig paid $15,000!

That means, Sonia's book and aligned programs led to $24,500 in paid speaking gigs.

So, Sonia profited $144,387 in her first year as an authorpreneur.

Breaking 6 figures isn't bad for her first year as an authorpreneur!

Plus, Sonia is now confident enough to raise her rates for workshops, speaking gigs, and coaching.

Now, Sonia is writing a second book where she will implement the same strategies to double her annual income. Plus, she plans to seek out more speaking and workshop opportunities and already has amazing referrals in place based on the five she was invited to lead last year.

Sonia sets her own schedule. She has the flexibility and freedom she desires. And she occasionally coaches from a hammock overlooking the ocean. Not bad, eh?

Sonia is living her authorpreneur dream life.

Exercise:

Brainstorm 3 aligned programs, including one for each price range, along with a flywheel constant that keeps readers/clients involved and connected. As a bonus, take a risk and dream up one big ticket item!

Funnel Entry: Free

Low Cost: $25ish book

Medium Cost: ($200-$300)

High Cost: ($1,500-$4,000)

Bonus Luxury Cost: ($10,000+)

Flywheel:

Exercise:

Now get into the details. Make a column for each of the offerings in your funnel and flywheel and list what exactly is needed to make them happen. Do you need to create a website? Upgrade your Zoom account? Set up an email list? Begin reaching out to potential clients? Write copy and design graphics for each offering? Create landing pages?

Whatever it is, add it to your To-Do List and get that first medium-cost offering out there so that when your book launches, it's waiting for readers to register!

Articulating your dream writer life, grappling with your money mindset, and formulating a solid funnel and flywheel of programming that aligns with the WHY and WHAT of your book are pivotal in actualizing your dream authorpreneur life. And you've done that!

Congratulations!

Now it's time to get your calendar back out and grab your favorite color highlighter (IRL or virtual). Remember all those doable due dates on your writing calendar and one-year marketing plan? Well, it's time to apply that same method to your funnel and flywheel. All these ideas are great, but without doable due dates affixed to them, you simply have a lot of notes on a page of a book. So, return to your final doable due date—your publication date—and begin adding the launches of each element of your funnel and flywheel to your calendar.

Set goals, while simultaneously giving yourself grace. And use the lists from the last exercise to help set realistic, bite-sized goals rather than simply listing something like "launch course" on the calendar. Each small step necessary for launching the course should be added to your calendar to make the process more doable.

Exercise:

Add your doable due dates for your funnel and flywheel to your calendar. Create a highlight reel in the space below, organizing major goals into months.

Funnel and Flywheel Timeline:

Month 1:

Month 2:

Month 3:

Month 4:

Month 5:

Month 6:

Month 7:

Month 8:

Month 9:

Month 10:

Month 11:

Month 12:

Now it's time to get to work on that To-Do List, making your dream authorpreneur life possible.

You've got this.

If you require some additional support and resources in manifesting your dream authorpreneur life, fear not. Tehom Center Publishing is ready to help. We offer 1:1 coaching and group cohorts that include the Book DreamMaker Authorpreneur program, providing real life strategies for making your funnel and flywheel plans a reality, including connections with web designers, social media specialists, business coaches, and other experts with aligned values sure to make your book and business thrive.

www.tehomcenter.org

Now pause to flip back through the entire Book DreamMaker Authorpreneur chapter of this handbook. Make a note of the exercises that excited you and the ones you found challenging. Where are you most proud? What item on your myriad lists ignites your imagination with creative potential? Where did you struggle most? Where do you still have questions?

Marginalized writers deserve more joy, self-care, and celebration in our lives, so don't move on without acknowledging what you've accomplished thus far. Truly. Call or text a colleague to brag about yourself. Toast a glass of wine or mix a mocktail. Turn on your favorite playlist and have a dance party. Go to the spa. Meet a friend at your favorite restaurant. Treat yourself. Whatever it might be, revel in the joy of completing the Book DreamMaker portion of *The Authorpreneur Handbook.*

Exercise:

In the space below, write down or draw how you're going to celebrate all you have accomplished in this chapter of The Authorpreneur Handbook thus far. Then...celebrate!

Now join me in saying this affirmation aloud.
"I am an authorpreneur. I deserve the life of my dreams. I will make those dreams a reality."
May it be so.

Aligning With Your Activism
A Ministerial Moment

"Language can be used as a means of changing reality."

— *Adrienne Rich*

I know that many, many marginalized people have suffered tremendous trauma at the hands of religion, including yours truly. Whether it's the demand for subservience, being called a hell-bound abomination, sacred texts justifying enslavement, mental illness referred to as demon possession, or the myriad other ways religious traditions have created harm for entire swaths of marginalized folks. In fact, many of Tehom Center Publishing's authors have written books about precisely this. If you are a person who has been so harmed by religion that any discussion of it is triggering for you, I invite you to skip this brief interlude and simply move to the conclusion. Institutional religion continues to hurt countless marginalized people every day, and I don't want this handbook to contribute to that in any way.

Still, many of the authors I coach stem from Tehom Center Publishing's Ministry from the Margins Books program, which gathers together marginalized ministers from around the world for the coaching featured in this book and aids in publishing their books that will transform the church and world. Because there are myriad marginalized ministers and activists who choose to remain within institutional religion to be agents of change. Often on the edge, the fringe, the margins of faith, spirituality, or religion, some marginalized ministers remain committed to their wisdom traditions because they are rooted in social justice and love, and their callings are to make that justice and love available to all people. So, they stay to be an activist from within. A subversive saint and scribe.

If this is how you identify, this interlude is specifically for you. It applies to activists, as well, because both ministers and activists often use the language of calling or vocation to describe why we do what we do. It all goes back to that initial WHY statement and the movement building Pauli Murray (also an activist and clergy) spoke of.

The reality is that *most* churches and most systems are entrenched in the white supremacist cisheteropatriarchy that continues to oppress the already marginalized. But, as Adrienne Rich reminds us, our language can be used as a means of changing reality. That is precisely what your book is doing. It's changing the reality of most churches, spiritualities, and systems.

So, I invite you to consider the ways in which the authorpreneur life *is* your ministry, your calling, your vocation, your activism. Your book—and living the authorpreneur life—is the means by which you change reality. Your book is your ministry. Marketing your book is evangelism, not so much focused on converting heathens or other notions grounded in colonization and crappy theology, but in the sense that your book is sharing "the good news" of transformational change. The programs aligned with your book that fund your authorpreneur life are your activism.

And you deserve to be fairly compensated for your ministry and activism.

Full stop.

No debate.

Aligning With Your Activism

Exercise:

In the space below, write and reflect on the ways in which your book, your book's marketing, and your authorpreneur life IS your ministry, activism, calling, and vocation. Whether there is a higher power, religious institution, or any external being doing the calling isn't as important as your inner conviction that your book—and the life and business you create in alignment with your book—is a manifestation of your vocation.

Conclusion

"Writing saved me from the sin and inconvenience of violence."

— *Alice Walker*

Writers from the margins deserve to live abundant, thriving, financially sustainable lives. YOU deserve abundance! And the world deserves to hear our stories, to read our books, to experience the transformations we offer. The authorpreneur life of your dreams is within your grasp and now that you've completed *The Authorpreneur Workbook*, you have the roadmap for getting you there!

And here's the great news. You can repeat this workbook every time you write a book, using it as a template for writing and marketing your book and then leveraging your book to elevate your business and brand.

Now that you've completed *The Authorpreneur Handbook*, you have A LOT of lists, doable due dates, highlight reels, and strategic plans for writing, marketing, and launching your funnel. I'll admit that it is a lot to manage and can become a bit overwhelming. To aid you in streamlining your process, I've narrowed all these fabulous exercises into a simple one-pager that you can glance at and be reminded of the big picture of your book and business.

Conclusion

You can download it simply at www.tehomcenter.org/handbook.

Download and print it. Fill it in and hang it where you write as a visual and tangible reminder of your revolutionary work. If it enlivens you, helps hold you accountable, or empowers you to celebrate your hard work, snap a selfie with it and share it on social media with #authorpreneurhandbook.

Once you've done that, it's time to reflect and celebrate!

Exercise:

Take a moment to flip back through the workbook to see how far you've come. Note below some of your standout moments, exercises you're especially proud of, or breakthroughs you don't want to forget.

Conclusion

Revolutionary writer, you deserve to be proud! Writing, publishing, and marketing a book, and then developing an entire business plan that shares your book's mission with the world is a really big deal. Be sure to celebrate this achievement in a major way! Take a nap, pop some bubbly, boogie to your favorite tunes, brag about yourself on social media, call your best friend to celebrate, relax in a bubble bath, attend a drag brunch, book a beautiful writing retreat, or do whatever you want to do to celebrate that you've taken a massive step toward creating your dream author life. Truly. You deserve it.

You now have all the tools for the authorpreneur life at your disposal. If you, like so many writers, need additional support, encouragement, accountability, and resources along the way, know that Tehom Center Publishing is here for you. We are a press publishing feminist and queer authors, with a commitment to elevate BIPOC writers. If you are an author living at the margins as a woman, queer person, BIPOC, or person living with disabilities, feel free to submit your book for possible publication with us by following the submission process on our website: www.tehomcenter.org

We do not charge authors to publish. Publishing with Tehom Center is absolutely free. We do realize that many, many authors need some help along the way, so we also offer equitable coaching programs empowering authors in

1. Book Writing
2. Book Marketing
3. Authorpreneurship

These coaching programs can be one-on-one or in one of our group cohorts. There are some writers who can brave the writing and publishing journey alone and have access to all the resources necessary for making their books thrive. This is not usually the case for marginalized authors. We often need additional coaching, access to resources otherwise withheld, and a community of like-minded writers to support, encourage, and hold us accountable.

Together, we thrive. This is what we're doing at Tehom Center Publishing. We are empowering the marginalized to live the authorpreneur lives of our dreams. Won't you join us?

Now, repeat after me: *"I am an authorpreneur. I deserve the life of my dreams. I am making those dreams a reality."*